MW01526625

MY WORLD OF DR.

Wow with my dream world because I truly do not know where to begin. Lord have mercy because the guns are aiming. Therefore, no; I will not go there. Listening to: ***AMBUSH IN THE NIGHT* by Bob Marley.** Thus; *many leaders fight for power without knowing what they are fighting for.*

Many kill; have radical ideals; idiotology. Yes, I know idiotology is not a word therefore, humans are governed by idiots. Idiot politicians; political leaders; presidents, and prime ministers, army generals; dictators that leave the citizens of their land raped and abused mentally, physically, and spiritually.

Idiots that cut your life short in the physical world and literally take away your life in the spiritual realm.

LION PAW

LION POWER

Listen people; the more you fight, the longer you stay in hell and burn.

The more you hate, the more the demons of hell truly love you.

The more you go against life, the further life moves away from you. Thus; demons favour humans because humans keep demons fed literally.

Spiritual thwarting is so not good, but this is the reality of the good and true. Therefore, I refuse to fight for power or, aid anyone who seek power and control.

I do not seek control, and I refuse to let those that run the government, religion, the different corporations of the globe control me.

You do not want, or like to be controlled, so why want to control others? Am I your child that you can brainwash, and lie to?

I refuse to let you control me, and belittle me.
I refuse to let you cause me to hate who I am; _**Black.**_

I refuse to let you tell me to hate my naturally kinky hair, and accept your hair; what you say is hair. My hair is God given; where did yours come from? And yes, I am being racist.

I refuse to number my hair because my hair cannot be numbered; it's real not fake.

I refuse to let you tell me to bleach my skin to look like you. I am Black, and that is who I shall, and will forever be. I do not want, or need to be White like you because I know what the colour of your skin represent. Therefore, _**SPIRITUAL DEATH AND FINAL DEATH IS WHITE.**_ Therefore, I truly do not need, or want to be dead like you.

**When I bleach my skin to look like you, I give up all rights to life.** Therefore telling God, I relinquish life because Death; Spiritual Death is my God. Therefore, I truly need to be me. I truly do not need to be apart of your wicked, and evil agenda; the living, breathing, and walking dead.

I KNOW THE WORTH OF DEATH THUS; DEATH KILLS PHYSICALLY, AND SPIRITUALLY.

Why should I be my brothers, and sisters enemy because of you?

Why should I let you bring your bullshit of war and strife in my world, and kingdom?

You don't know me, and I truly don't want, or need to know you.

You have no intelligence thus, you educate in lies; get others to accept, and live by your lies and deceit. Thus humans globally lack intelligence when it comes to White People, and the lies they educate in, spread, get you to accept, and more.

Whites lack intelligence, and moral values thus; the world we live in is in such chaos; turmoil.

Many want to be White without knowing the cost, and tricks of them.

Once again and therefore, *the White Race globally lack intelligence; good and true knowledge; moral values.* Therefore, what the *TRUE BLACK RACE KNOW; THE WHITE RACE CANNOT KNOW, AND WILL NEVER EVER KNOW.* Still don't know until this day, and it matters not if you read all my books. You still cannot know what I know because, it's not all that I know I can give.

AFRICA UNITE – Bob Marley, but Black People still cannot learn; refuse to learn. Therefore, many Blacks has and have forgotten the life; truth

3

within them. Thus many forfeit life. Has and have become WHITE.

I truly do not care if you like me. I have life; what do you have?

You want power and control thus, you try to make yourselves be God, but not one of you can be God. You are all nasty thus; God is truly not with any of you.

Your God is death, and this is why you literally look like death; spiritual death; the dead. You kill, and create strife for power yet, the power you seek evil cannot attain, will never ever attain because life is truly not ignorant; dumb, illiterate. And none of you come with your racism bullshit on my part, or I will tell you literally to your face to eat shit and die.

The colour of your skin to not make you Black. This is why I teach; some Whites are Black – fall under the Black Banner of Life, and some Blacks are White – fall under the White Banner of Death. Therefore; when some Blacks say they are White, do not slander them, or belittle them. They are telling you the truth. They are physically, and spiritually dead. Apart of the White Race of Death literally.

WAR – BOB MARLEY

Humanity; humans truly need to listen to the lyrics of this song.

Sorry everyone this is a dream book, and I am off track already.

It's July 10, 2019, and wow for my dream world because; my dream world is graphic when it comes to death.

NATURAL MYSTIC – Bob Marley

Dreamt the past. I truly do not know what dreaming in the past represent. I am so no sure if the past represent future fighting thus; I give you: ***NATURAL MYSTIC by Bob Marley. Yes, I can go back into the past via my dream world, this is truly not impossible for me,*** but I truly do not know about you. My world is different from yours thus I see differently. Listen to the song because Bob did say; ***"many more will have to suffer, many more will have to die."***

Like I said, I dreamt the past. White People; dressed in Roman attire with helmets and swords, as well as spears.

Men and women were fighting. It was as if Romans were; no, not it's not like it was as if. Romans and or, White Women and men were fighting each other. In the dream you could see the spears that some threw to kill the others; ***their own people.*** Twice in the dream I saw the slitting of someone's throat. Therefore, I truly do not know why my dream world is becoming so graphic; me seeing someone's throat being slit.

I will not analyze this dream because I truly do not know what this dream represent.

I do not know what the slitting of throats represent either.

I do not know what spears represent. No, that's not true. ***Spears represent the death of evil in the spiritual realm.*** So yes, the White Race is slowly dying; being eliminated in the spiritual realm.

My other dream entailed the hospital. I was at this hospital, and Kirk Douglas was sitting by himself. Family and people, he looked so frail and disgusting that wow to how disgusting he looked.

After seeing the ugliness of this man, I saw his son Michael Douglas. He was now beside his father. Kirk Douglas asked me something to do with children, and I tried explaining to him about this, but he did not believe me, but I did not care because I told him the truth.

In life; people. No one can live in sin and expect to die right, and go to the kingdom and abode of God. This is impossible. ***If you live wrong, you must die wrong.***

If you are not of truth, then you are not of God. You are of Death therefore; many people die to see Death. This is a given here on earth.

After my conversation with Kirk Douglas, I was on my way, trying to find my way out of the hospital and having a hard time of it. The hospital was huge. I went in one direction, and saw White People dying.

I went another way; in another direction, and saw sick White People. Trust me, I was lost in this hospital.

I truly will not analyze this dream because I don't want to know. Too much sickness, and death for my liking plus; I was lost in the midst of all this. So not good for me.

My other dream entailed Alicia Keys.

Alicia and I were getting married. She was dressed in a beautiful wedding dress. She had a train; long train that was not attached to the dress. No, that's not right. The train was different. Not polka dots, but little green balls was on the train/jacket. It was so elegant that I wanted a dress like that with a train to how beautiful the dress was.

See the wedding was different; not your traditional wedding. She Alicia walked before me, and I was behind her. Trust me the train was long. Going in behind Alicia she stood by this man who I thought was her father because he was black, and a bit chubbier than a normal built man. I think he was in a gray suit, and he was not pleased in the dream that Alicia and I were getting married.

Standing beside Alicia I held her hand.

After that because; I did not witness Alicia, and I/me exchanging vows. *After holding her hand, I left to go prepare for the reception at the house.*

Going to go prepare food for the people, Alicia joined me. She was no longer in her wedding attire. *We were in this place that looked like a black and or, dark sea that was frozen over.* The area we were was not dark as the outer area. Where we were, the ice was circular and white, and I began to sing, and Alicia joined me in singing. I was singing Hallelujah, and Alicia chimed in on the Hallelujah. Then she added Jesus in the mix of the song. The odd part of the dream for me was; not so much the dark black sea that was frozen over, but in the distance to the right of me; *this above medium built Black Woman dressed in red was frozen in the dark sea water.* You saw her from the waist up, and she too was singing. Trust me, I will not analyze this dream because I truly do not know what this dream means. All I know is; dark sea water is not good. I cannot tell you what the frozen black water represent. Thus, I just have to watch and see what water destruction devastate the United States.

Green I know is disappointment. As for the wedding, we just have to see who dies in her family literally.

You know what; let me let it go because that dream; all my dreams were not good dreams. Death is surrounding me more and more therefore, I see a lot of death in my dream world.

Yes I had more dreams, but I cannot remember them.

So until another day, do take care.

And not one of you better come to me and say, you should not have said that about Kirk Douglas. I saw what I saw, and his death is not pretty, it's ugly. If only some of you can see the death of some like I can. I do not just see the dead; how people are going to die in dreams. At times when I close my eyes, I see how people are going to die, and it's not pretty. Thus sometimes I wonder if I am the Death Angel because I see so much death.

There is the abode of God; Life, and there is the abode of Death; the dead. I know both realms therefore, I know life and death.

I know creation, and how life came into being.

I can tell you about hell because I see hell; know who are hell bound literally.

I know the stench of death, and can smell the stench of death. Some people before they die; if they are wicked and evil, they die bad, and the stench of filth – poop, kaka surrounds them before they die. They cannot smell their stench; the stench of their death, but you can. Some, you see the grotesque look of them. Therefore, if you watch a grotesque movie – deformed people in the worse sense, you get an idea of what some people look like before they die. No, I cannot draw, and if I could draw; I would draw the faces of the people who I see that is going to die literally, and those who are going to die bad, but I am glad I cannot draw. Seeing so much death not just in your dreams, but in your waking state do wreak havoc on your psyche – your physical, and mental health.

I cannot speak for others who can see the dead, but some dead find me, and hold on to me literally. Yes, they see their hell, and want me to save them from hell therefore, they find me, and hold on to me, and I've told you this in some of my earlier books.

I know the confines of hell thus, I truly do not know why people would want to die to go to hell.

I've told you, hell has no air conditioners. ***You created your own hell, and God cannot send any of his, and her children into hell to save anyone. LIFE AND DEATH ARE NOT THE SAME. Just as death cannot go into the abode of God, God cannot go into the abode of hell.***

It's a stupid man, woman, or child that believe God let his and or, her own child die to save the wicked and evil. ***NO CHILD OF GOD CAN DIE BECAUSE THEY ARE OF THE TRUTH.***

THEREFORE, ***TRUTH CANNOT DIE.***

Lies, sin cause you to die, and billions are slated to die due to sin.

THERE IS NO JESUS BANK ACCOUNT WITH GOD. However, ***THERE IS A SIN ACCOUNT WITH DEATH*** thus I tell you in other books; *to know your life, and death.* *See your good and evil deeds.*

I've told you in other books, if God made his child die to save humans; the wicked and evil then, God would be a bitch nigger. God would have bowed, and succumbed to Death, and the will of Death. Therefore; God was Death's bitch because, God made sacrifices unto death also. But because I know God; Life, I know God would never ever sacrifice anyone whether good, or evil to death.

True life know not death hence true life cannot die. True life can only live. So truly know the lie that was told on God. Man made God out to be Death's bitch, and not one of you are seeing this. Therefore, millions; hundreds of millions; billions were educated falsely by the deceived; the true demons of Earth; yes, Satan's children.

In my homeland some of say; if a man; person don't like you, they will give you basket to carry water. The statement is self explanatory. Thus, the hatred of many in the White Race – so called Jews – White Jews. They hated your ass therefore, they lied to you thus, their so called holy book – man's so called holy bible of lies, and deceit.

Yes, the bible is death's book but tell some of you this; you revolt, and throw up the hate flag right away. Therefore, as man is dirty; their god is dirty as well. Thus, the true and living god cannot be the God of man because, the true and living god is not dirty, nor does the true and living god deal in filth; the filth, and nastiness of man. As for the Alicia Keys dream. I do not know if it's New York, or Los Angeles that is going to have problems environmentally. The frozen black water people.

Wow, because the Black Women in red that was frozen in the water I truly do not know.

THREE LITTLE BIRDS – *Bob Marley,* but I know everything is truly not going to be alright for many; billions.

Michelle

It's early morning July 13, 2019, and I have to wonder about the state of young black people.

Why are they so stupid when it comes to gun violence?

Why is it that they would rather shatter the hopes, and dreams of the Black Race? *(Based on hue, and excluding Babylonian Indians).*

Why do they need acceptance from anyone including gangs?

Are street creds that precious to them that they care not for who they rob, and kill?

WHY IS IT THAT MUSIC HAS BECOME THE KILLING FIELD, KILLING GAME, AND END GAME FOR SOME?

When you listen to some rap music, and the way they glorify killing; it amazes me to the state of the Black Race. We are the ones killing self, and we are not seeing this.

We glorify all that is wicked and evil, and think it's a game. We are killing our own race, and no one is talking about it. *All has, and have changed in the music game; industry because, RAPPERS HAS, AND HAVE BECOME GLORIFIED KILLERS; MURDERERS OF SELF, THE BLACK COMMUNITY, BLACK RACE, AND OTHERS GLOBALLY.*

We have no sense of pride hence; Black communities globally have, and has become dysfunctional.

Yes, this is my rant this morning. Did I dream about snakes this week?

Yes

It's like; no, it's not like. In my dream, I was somewhere, and I saw this White Man. He was in a tree with this huge snake. He was petting and or, trying to capture the snake. Think anaconda like snake to how big the body of the snake was. Then, I was in this pit. Huge pit. It was like a party, no not party, music was playing, and this one young black girl in blue shorts put her hand down her shorts, and I believe a snake came to her side. I so can't remember. Anyway, I laid down to sleep, and snakes were around me. This tiny one came on the bed, and I bax it off. Only to find out this week someone I know. A young DJ got held up at gun point by masked robbers. That hurt me so much when I found out. Therefore, I have to truly wonder about the state of Black People especially; young Black Men to how violent, and disrespectful they have become.

WE AS BLACK PEOPLE ARE THE ONE TEARING EACH OTHER DOWN.

WE AS BLACK PEOPLE ARE THE ONES DAMAGING OUR OWN BLACK STATE, BLACK MIND, BLACK PEOPLE, BLACK CHILDREN, BLACK COMMUNITY, AND MORE.

We are a jealous, and nasty set of people because; we cannot, and do not want to see our own Blacks rise positively.

Our mind is set in this stinking, and rotten mind set that we cannot see the damage we are causing self, and others. Yes, I wanted to cry when I heard what happen, so I just held on to him, the young DJ in real life and said, *do not stop rising.* When you are successful; rising, other Blacks do not want to see you rise, or prosper. ***Do not let these thugs take your prosperity from you. Keep going, do not give up.*** Karma is a bitch when it comes back to haunt them. Do not do a thing to hurt anyone because you are well known, continue going.

Therefore, life's a bitch when your own Black People do all to tear you down.

Music is not a game yet, many in the music industry use music to promote evil; violence.

And I will say this; *the community you live in did not create you. You created the negative environment you live in. You created a negative environment for self, so truly do not blame the community; blame you; the negative environment you, and others created for self.*

The poor state Blacks are in is due to Blacks. I will not, and refuse to accept the slave and or, slavery mindset, or mentality. We as a people, and nation can rise but; ***how many want to truly rise in a good, and true way?***

Negativity begets negativity, and evil begets evil; death. Both the same yes, thus many who live in their negative; evil mindset.

As Blacks we are our own destruction, and it's sad how we are destroying self.

It's sad how wi living. Therefore, I am going back to the Cherine Anderson, and her song:

HOW WE LIVING

Backwards thinking
Backwards mentality
Backwards living

Begets backwards, and regressive people with regressive and or, poor mentality; thinking, thieving, and deadly lifestyle. Therefore, many young Blacks are strapped, ready to kill at will without thinking of the damage they are causing to their own Black People; Race; Black Community.

WE ARE FREE yet, the choices we make; makes you think about the mentality, and state of Blacks globally.

Therefore:

BACKWARDS THINKING BEGETS BACKWARDS PEOPLE WITH GHETTO MENTALITY.

A mentality that is so stink; it kills.

Like I said; we are the ones to be blamed for our poor thinking; mentality, and absolutely no one can come to me with slavery.

We want to be slaves therefore, we buy into the negative systems given to us by our political leaders, religious leaders, gang members and or, affiliates, negative friends, including family. As humans we do not think for self because; for billions the negative state they live in suits them just fine. And yes, you will not comprehend this because humans are controlled in many ways; told how to think; therefore, billions cannot think for self. Psychology, and the different psychological thinking including the different media outlets; advertising you are bombarded with on television, radio, billboards, the internet, and more. Therefore, advertising is a part of psychological conditioning; brainwashing. It does affect your thinking; the way you perceive things whether good, or bad.

Yes, I am glad the young DJ, and his friend is okay and whomever did this, you will have hell to pay literally. This you can take to the bank guaranteed.

Did I dream Tessanne Chin earlier this week?

Yes.

She was on a talk show in the dream, and she was talking about Seaga, and how he was buried in Hero's Park, and everyone was happy. Trust me, in the dream my spirit was vexed. I could not watch the interview to how upset I was. In the dream I said, they should have never buried him in Hero's Park. ***I would have just dash wey di bady.*** Meaning, would have buried him in a regular cemetery because he's no damned hero. Trust mi, *di bitch dey a hell where he belongs.* Yes, many Jamaicans are going to be upset, but I truly do not give a F. Most of them; the people of Jamaica put their corrupt, nasty, and stinking politicians above self, and God. ***They run behind these dungs of shit like they are gods,*** and treat them like gods. Therefore, the backwards mentality, and thinking of a; ***BACKWARDS,***

16

**AND REGRESSIVE NATION.** People who do not have any dyam sense. Therefore, the political leaders of Jamaica can feed the people shit, and they gobble up the shit, nyam the shit, and wipe dem mouth like a good food they are getting. And absolutely none of you the educated dunce of Jamaica better not say anything because, all of you know this is true. Some a unnu pee pee cluck cluck behine unnu politician tu. Dyam ass – ediat. Think for self. Look at the poor state Jamaica is in.

Yes the Bulla talk come to mind.
Dyam licky licky, and wanga gut.

Look at the crime rate of Jamaica.

Stop with the slave mentality, and think for self.
Do better for self.

No, none of you can because; _**you're all dry roots; dead**_. Therefore, unnu sell out Marcus Garvey for rice – food. Now tell me; _**what does that say for the lots of you?**_

**You do not want, or need to be educated in positive growth, positive thinking, positive commerce, positive self, positive wealth, health, and more. Unnu want to be shit therefore, unnu politicians treat unnu like shit literally.**

Onwards I go because I am getting pissed.

Morons think because your life is worth it. Stop letting your political leaders turn unnu inna..no unnu a idiots already therefore, unnu a literal falla batty.

Family and People, my true family. *Yu think a now hell want him; Seaga!!!!!!*

Truss mi when mi tell yu, hell has, and have been waiting for his soul, and spirit literally therefore, I told you about this in one of my very early books. ***Laade have mercy because di beating wey im a get; it's a wonder how people in the living not hearing his cries literally. Bitch dey a hell thus, one less demon spirit the world have to worry about literally.***

No Lovey, these wutless/wotless Jamaicans that run behind their political leaders like dem a anything special. *Then when things go bad you hear;*

WE WANT JUSTICE.

Dummy, no one can have justice in an unjust world. A world governed by the unjust; wicked and evil.

Look at the state of Jamaica Lovey.

Look at the way the people think.
Look at how they are killing each other.

JAMAICA – JA – MAICA means; GOD MADE ME.

You made the people Lovey thus the *FLAG OF LIFE – JAMAICAN FLAG* that they disrespect, and cannot hold in high esteem. They treat the flag of life, and country like dung hence; Jamaica is a killing field, and the pedophile capital of the world. Therefore, some family members, willingly, and knowingly sell their children for prophet whoops, profit; money. Yes, the Roman Catholic Church is the pedophile organization of the globe because, pedophiles are protected, and yes, Lovey I know you have absolutely nothing to do with religion. *YOU DO NOT RELY ON MAN; HENCE, MAN LIE ON YOU, AND USE YOU AS THEIR FRONT TO DO EVIL UNTO MAN; HUMANS; EACH OTHER.*

But Lovey, the children that are abused. But then again, humans condone the shit of their priests, and political leaders globally therefore, *HUMANS ACCEPT, AND CONDONE EVIL FOR SELF; THEIR WAY OF LIVING.*

Oh man, I am so off track because this is a dream book.

Did I dream I was at my dad's place earlier on this week?

Yes, and in the dream he bought me 3 – 4 loaves of bread; white bread, and they were all spoilt. Had mold on them. And on that note I am so going to close this part of the book.

Michelle

Oh man have I been lazy when it comes to my dreams, and in all honesty, I don't want to write about them anymore. I dream a lot, and see a lot.

In this part of the book I am not going to go in-depth with my dreams because some I cannot. They are vague which is truly good for me.

I will not analyze these dreams either because; at times I analyze wrong. You can analyze them for self and or, for me.

This dream I did not want to put into this book because it has to do with the English Monarch, and I truly do not care about them. The majority of them need to get a damned job like regular hard working citizens that work, and pay taxes.

My YouTube is so not working, and I am not going to worry about it. Bell has always been shit, and will forever be shit to me when it comes to internet access, and speed. You pay so much for internet access, and get shit. Their service is shit. Plus if you need to get a Wi-Fi boost, you have to buy and or rent their pods, and you can't have one, you have to have four in your apartment to amplify the signal. So you're paying more money out for an already shitty service.

Thus I am going to be racist here; **_White People's technology is shit period._** We pay for shit hence, our elevated stress level when it comes to their so called shitty technology that gouge your pocket because; **_corporations are profit driven, and nothing else._**

You pay for everything including the paper they send your bill on. You know what let me stop because, I will get rattled up. So yes, my internet is so not working properly, and I cannot get unto YouTube, and I am so not going to worry about it. I have my games on my Tab E that I play.

Getting back to my dream because I've wasted so much of your valuable time chattering, and still chattering.

Oh yes, the British Monarch.

Saw on MSN a picture of Meagan Markle, and Harry meeting with Beyoncé and Jay Z for the premiere of the Lion King. Meagan was in black, and I so do not know why I picked up on this in my dream world. In my dream Meagan and Harry was in the same outfit they wore for the Lion King premiere. But in the dream; when Megan and Harry met Beyoncé and Jay Z they shook hands, and Beyoncé and Jay Z went through this tall door; you know those ancient looking doors in the movies that you would use two hands to open at the same time? Well this was the door. So, Beyoncé and Jay Z went through those doors, and as soon as Beyoncé and Jay Z went through this door; the door quickly closed leaving Meagan, and Harry outside. Trust me; *the door shut tight.* Meagan and Harry could not get in, and you could see the distraught, no not distraught but when the door closed it was not pretty. Meagan and Harry looked so lonely…not wanted, and by themselves. After seeing that; all you had was empathy for Meagan, and Harry.

After that; I was seeing inside where Jay Z, and Beyoncé were. They were walking, and Jay Z looked backed. He was shocked and or, surprised that the door shut so fast behind him, and Beyoncé, and Meagan and Harry was not let in. Beyoncé was not surprised. She kept a cool head, and kept walking because; *the LOCK OUT OF MEAGAN AND HARRY HAD TO DO WITH HER.* She was the one to cause Meagan, and Harry to be locked out.

I will not analyze this dream because I know what this dream mean. The Priestess of Death is just exercising her right of passage; who they accept, and decline in their *NEW WORLD ORDER.* Figure it out.

Therefore, for many Satan rule. Let me leave it there because like I said I will not analyze my dreams. I already know the meaning of this dream like I said.

Many of you truly do not know certain things hence; *YOU TRULY DO NOT KNOW YOUR BOOK OF THE DEAD; DAMNED WHICH IS YOUR SO CALLED HOLY BIBLE.*

I know some of you say King James was Black, and I am so not going to get into the lineage of the Monarch of England. I will leave it alone because they truly do not concern me. Thus, the Book of Death. *Damn, the Black King that Revelations talked about. I know who he is.*

This other dream had to do with me on a bus. The bus driver was light skinned, tall, and he had dreams but did not know what they represented. When I got off the bus the door closed then opened, and I told him that a cousin in a dream could represent a brother, or sister in your dream world. The odd part of the dream though was the door kept opening, and closing. I wanted to tell him more but did not get the opportunity to. Therefore, I have to do a book on dream representation.

I wanted to tell this man about evil representation. I know I talked about this briefly in one of my earlier books. *In the dream world, evil is represented in many ways.*

For example, say you know someone in the living is evil; truly evil. Your dream world will use that person to show you that evil is around you, or evil is trying to hurt you, or if you like someone, and the person you like is evil; your dream world will show you this by using the evil person that you know. And I know this is a poor explanation, but certain things are hard for me to explain.

I will not analyze the Meagan Markle, Harry, Beyoncé, and Jay Z dream because I truly know what the dream mean, and represent.

There are certain things I know thus Nimrud and or, Nimrod for some is real for me. You will not comprehend this because you truly do not know the **_KINGDOM OF THE DEAD; SATAN LIKE I DO._** I see, and know people hence; I know the power evil seeks.

Anyway, true life must go on.

My other dream had to do with water and this huge fish and or, something in the water that was eating, hurting and or, killing people. The dream is so vague I truly cannot remember it fully.

Dreamt about Fred Hammond, and his stubbornness. Stubborn are you. Listen, people; my true family. **_If God is waring you about something, truly listen._** My beliefs are not Christian because; I truly have no beliefs when it comes to God for whom I call Lovey. I have a true, and personal relationship with God that is not based on religion but truth, solid trust, doubt, true love, and more. **_I know God therefore, I cannot believe. Knowledge is not the same as belief._** Once you know God you cannot believe, you have to continue knowing. Belief changes, but knowledge can never change thus I tell you, and will forever tell you to; **_know God._**

God cannot lie but man lie; humans lie each and every day, every second of the day for some.

23

God cannot go back on his, and her world therefore, _**know who God is.**_

**If you believe in the lies of men that's fine. This is your true right, but know, you cannot know God based on the lies of men, or anyone including the bible.**

GOD CANNOT GO BACK ON HIS, AND HER WORD.

For some God is female, and for some God is male, but for me God is both when it comes to the physical, and spiritual, but for those who truly know; God is genderless in the purest of form. This is where energy comes in, and _**if you don't know how energy works; you cannot know how God work in many ways.**_ Therefore, _**truth is imperative to life.**_ Yes along the way many have fallen short of this due to lies; beliefs, but like I said; your belief is your right. I am not here to change anyone because as humans when it comes to God, we are to know better.

**We can no longer put God on our dirty shelf as self.**

**We can no longer make God out to be dirty, and a giver backer taker.**

**God is not like man therefore, we cannot treat God like we treat our self; dirty.**

If you are getting a good message that say take care of your health; take care of your health. There is something there that you truly do not know.

No my true family. I cannot be bothered with people. No, I cannot be bothered with holier than thou Christians that think they know it all, and that they have God. Christian that think if you do not have Jesus you are not of God. And I am going to say this again in this book. ***GOD IS NOT DEATH'S BITCH. GOD DO NOT MAKE SACRIFICES UNTO DEATH.***

LIFE AND DEATH IS NOT THE SAME, and God would never ever let any of his and her children die to save the wicked and evil of this earth. YOU SINNED, YOU ARE RESPONSIBLE FOR YOUR OWN SINS. It is not fair, nor is it just for someone else to pay the penalty for you. God cannot hate any of his, or her own children; therefore, ***GOD TRULY DO NOT DEAL IN DEATH, AND THIS SOME OF YOU IN THE BLACK COMMUNITY NEED TO REALIZE.***

IF I HAVE SINNED AGAINST YOU, IT IS YOU THAT I NEED FORGIVENESS FROM. WHAT IS SO HARD IN SEEING THIS, AND KNOWING THIS?

Use your common sense.

Why the hell should God's child go to hell and burn like a bitch for something he, or she did not do?

I am not your bitch. I should not have to die for you. No one should come on now.

You sinned reckless and rude, go to hell for self. You burn. You did not truly love you; so you did, and you're still doing the bidding of hell. So stay in hell, I refuse to go there; hell for you.

No Lovey this is getting to me to see how unjust, and unfair humans are. We, and I am not going to take myself out of this because; I've sinned too. We sin, so why should someone else die to save us from our sins?

Why should that person, or anyone have to go down to see death because of the wrongs of others?

How fair and just are you Lovey when you cause this to happen?

Am I responsible for that person's sins if you have not given them unto me?

You've given me seeds and I've told you and wrote; *I am accountable for these seeds.* I have to ensure these seeds live right, *but if any go against truth, then they are on their own.* I've also told you, if I have educated wrong; falsely, do not hold that person accountable for living wrong if I have educated wrong. Hold me accountable because, I gave wrong; false. This is only fair. Some of my goodness must go towards paying down the debt of the good, and true seeds you've given me Lovey if any of them; those seeds have debt; sin in Death's record book.

Life isn't about religion, and sending people to hell, and this many Blacks cannot get because; *Jesus was instilled in them.* Many are banking on the Jesus Bank without knowing there is no Jesus Bank. *We are all held accountable for our sins, and absolutely no one who has died can have life.*

IF YOU ACCEPT DEATH IN THE LIVING, YOU MUST DIE TO SEE DEATH ONCE YOUR SPIRIT SHED THE FLESH.

***Death takes lives not life.* LIFE CANNOT KILL, NOR DO LIFE KILL.** Death kills yet, humans cannot see this; do not want to know this. All is centered around lies; the lies told, and handed down from generation unto generation, and no one wants to break away from these generational lies.

You know what Lovey, let me leave it. I did my part. I sent this man a book of what I saw. If he wants to be dyam stubborn let him be. ***IT JUST GOES TO SHOW YOU LOVEY THAT HUMANS ESPECIALY THOSE IN THE BLACK COMMUNITY, WILL ALWAYS LOOK FOR LIFE IN DEATH.*** Therefore, Death has become their god because; they truly do not know the difference between life, and death.

They truly do not know what it means to be a Jew; have good and true life.

Yes, man will never get the concept of Jew therefore, Juju Wata. If you are Jamaican figure it out, and know what Jew mean on a different yet simple level.

Yes, I know Juju for some represent evil. But mi a talk bout Juju Wata not evil. Every Jamaican should know what Juju Wata is, therefore, Jamaica stand for; *GOD MADE ME.* Thus every Jamaican has, and have forgotten what ***JA MAICA STAND FOR, AND REPRESENT.*** God gave us life, and Jamaicans destroyed their own life. Let me stop there because there is more dreams that I've had.

Dreamt Jennifer Lopez, and A. Rod. In the dream everything with them was like a game, and this pink line was eliminating everything. You now how in certain games like Candy Crush how you line up certain elements, and they would be eliminated in that row. Well this is how I saw them; Jennifer Lopez, and A. Rod. I will not analyze this dream

27

because I truly do not care about these people's life. And yes, my dream world would not let me go of them; It just kept showing me elimination when it comes to these two.

Yes, my family will truly not like these books when they know it's me writing them. Trust me; they will be so against me thus, the elimination in my family as well. But in all honesty people, I truly do not give a rats ass if my family disown me. I have God already so if they think severing ties with me is truly going to hurt, they can truly think again.

In life people; well my true family, ***you need to live to be by yourself.*** Many people cannot be by themselves, and this is so sad. Take the time to know you, and take the time to spend time with yourself; you. It is well worth it trust me.

Thinking about the Jennifer Lopez, and A. Rod dream. As women and men, we have to be careful with he message we are sending our children.

You know what let me be candid. ***Many of us have children, and some women use their vagina as a frigging bus terminal. As one man rush out, another park their bus in her.*** No, I am not throwing stones, but as parents both male, and female we have a legal obligation, and moral right as to how we teach our children, and live our life around them.

Therefore, many children live what they see. Mama shell dung di place, don't be surprised if pickney cum shell dung di place tu. ***If you do not have good moral values how can your child have good moral values?***

Yes, as parents we try to teach our children the right way, and some do not take telling this I know. ***But as parents, you have to value your home including your children, and what they see you do.***

Your legs, and penis cannot be an open door for everyone come on now.

Where is your child moral, and legal right to life?

Therefore, the world is in a mess. Many do sell their immoral values to the world; others.

I know there are more dreams, but I so cannot remember them.

So until another day, do take care.

Michelle

Oh lord I need to end this book. So don't want to write anymore. It's hot, and my body is like a furnace. Have a fan but it's so not cutting it right now. Oh well, so not going to worry about the heat. I just have to ensure my life is safe where my spirit, and I am going to say flesh truly do not end up in hell. Thus I write; if we cannot take the heat here on Earth, how are we going to take the heat in hell because; ***there are no air conditioners in hell.*** So in all I do, I need to protect myself from the confines; prisons of hell.

I truly do not know about you, but I refuse to strive to go to hell. Whether you know it or not, hell is real for billions. Onwards with my dreams because something is truly not right in my family. I won't even talk about my daughter because she an altogether other case.

I will leave her alone because, truth takes precedence in my life. If she does not want to adhere to the truth, and live by the truth; that's her problem. Shi too stubborn, and if she thinks she's hurting me in all she's doing she had better think again. When hell unleash on her, she cannot blame anyone but self. She is selfish, and dunkcya.

In all you do honey, you are not spiting me, you are spiting yourself. You are getting older, and it's in old age that retribution take some of you. The pain you feel is all on you. I learnt the hard way therefore, I am trying to teach you; secure your life from now because in old age; shit happens, and it's truly painful.

Talking about pain. Severe back pain is gone. Trust me, God is truly good. Yes, we say slow, but trust me, God is truly sure. I am slowly working on my health, and everything is falling into place.

Did my ultrasound of my breast again, and the lump was not there. The technician said, the lump isn't there; as if shocked. Listen everyone, I am truly happy it's not there. I was praying, and asking God to let everything be okay. Meaning heal me. While praying, I would touch the area the lump was. I would pray for my back as well, and positive things happened in my life thanks to God, and prayer. Now I have to continue to work on my health, and let God stay permanently in my life in a good way.

I so need a vacation. I need to go to Africa people. So hopefully by the end of the year into next year more than a positive miracle happen in my life where I get to go to Africa with Lovey.

It's July 19, 2019, and I dreamt I was on this space ship. These kids – _**white kids**_ stole a space ship, and I was on the ship they stole. When they did this; stole the space ship, all you saw was a fleet of space ships appeared, and open fire on us. We dodged the line of fire, but wow. This dream was like a movie for me because Toby McGuire from the Spider Man movies was involved.

I will not analyze this dream because like I said, it was like unto a movie. And to be perfectly honest, I told the Moon I was mad at it, and right after I had that dream – stolen space ship dream.

No family and people, I am vex. I am upset at the way countries have armies; pay people to kill. People do for death; cannot uphold the law, and laws of life, and these lands globally is truly not being punished in my view. Yes the environment of Earth has, and have changed, but I need to see more happen. Space need to take action as well. It's bad enough man; humans lie on the Moon saying; *MAN WALKED ON THE MOON.* Dyam lie.

Earth cannot have a heating system alone people. Earth need a cooling system, and the moon is our cooling system. So, if man cannot go to the sun, how are they going to go to the Moon?

The lies the White Race tell is truly beyond me. You know what; let's forget it because knowledge; right knowledge will always lead to the truth, and lies will always lead to death..

Right now humans are dying, and it's going to get worse.

I dreamt my dead mother therefore, something is so not right in this family. I need to call my brother and warn him, because someone a tief someone. You know what, I am so not going to worry about anything, let whomever the thief is; galang. Time truly langa dan rope. The dream had to do with my mother buying two homes, and her name was not on the land title. I had to tell her she did not own the house because her name was not on the title. In the dream, she had bought a house with Phillip, and he did not put her name on it. Therefore, at the end of the dream she was distraught, held her head down as if crying. She was in black, and the odd part of the dream was ***she had on long black eye lashes.*** I so will not analyze this dream because like I said, something is truly not right in my family. My daughter is doing shit she's not suppose to do, and my sister is doing shit she's not suppose to do. I cannot speak on the behalf of my cousins because I truly do not talk to them.

Laade have mercy because the dead; my dead mother is truly not pleased. So I will leave all to their own demise literally. I am not going to be the one to end up sorry in the end. Do you honey, and truly good luck to you in the end.

This afternoon, I had the most wonderful of sleep. Waking up, I thought of the Cayman Islands, and my cousin. ***It was as if the island is sinking.*** The water level is rising around the island, where the water reaches the homes inland. I am so not going to worry about the Cayman Islands because this island is truly not my concern. Yes, I am scared for my cousin, and just editing these few lines gives my stomach the butterflies.

Wow

Michelle

It's July 22, 2019, and I am so mad at my dream world. Good morning everyone. *I am so tired of my dream world literally. I am fed up of seeing into the lives of dirty people.* I need a change come on now.

Trust me, who needs a tabloid magazine when they have me; well these books.

Before this morning; I had other dreams from Friday, and lord have mercy I need to move away from some of my children to the shit in their life.

I so cannot take on the stress of anyone including the stress of my dream world anymore. Thus I am tired of Death, and the way Death is holding on to me physically, and spiritually including beyond.

Death and or, evil need a time extension, and I am oppose to this time extension here on earth, and in the spiritual realm including beyond. Death and or, evil had their 24000 years on earth, go to hell and die now cunyo. Your 24000 years is up. No time extension for you. Take your evil people, armies of death globally, diseases, diseased people, filthy economies of the globe, filthy, nasty, stink, and dirty people, nasty and stinking living, and more nasty things and go.

Take your nasty foods, and genetically modified foods, and people and go too. Truly don't need them here on Earth literally.

Leave me alone with wanting a time extension because I will never ever let evil get a time extension if I can help it.

34

I am tired of seeing death, and the ugliness of death, and sin come on now.

Dreamt an ex friend of my son. He was in my apartment at one time in one dream; then my other dream had to do with him having HIV, and the virus being undetectable in his system. I will not get into manmade diseases because these diseases are money for the pharmaceutical industry. Money for doctors who need to keep employed; you visiting them. Keep you the average citizen sick as well as; work for some of you the average citizen.

Therefore, life is about money for those who control the global economy.

For some this is population control, but in all honesty, population control is dead because man; humans are going to run out of land space real soon. Therefore; global food shortage and yes, rising death tolls. You know what let me stop because this is a dream book. Man a look to space to live.

Space cyaa grow food?
Dirt inna space?
Wata inna space?
Rivers and seas inna space?

Moon, and the Universe hold your peace, and true peace and stay quiet. I am trying to make a point here.

Energy, and the flow and power of energy I know hence, I know creation; thy power.

Dreamt my son and I went to the bank. The bank; my bank renovated, and for some strange reason I had a Comet container in my hand, and some of the content spilled on the floor of the bank. I did not realize until when one of the Black Bank Teller's showed me. The bank had majority black bank tellers. I sat in line to see the teller, but my son; first child ended up doing my bank transaction for me.

What was odd for me was this family; Arab and or, Middle Eastern to African family came out of this area in the bank. You saw the man, but his wives and kids were covered from head to toe in black. You could not see their faces because their face were fully covered. You couldn't even see their eyes. They were leaving the bank. In the dream it was TD Bank of Canada. Strange because I do not bank with TD. Therefore, I do not know what security breach is going to happen in one of Canada's bank, or a bank globally.

Black for me is truly not good and yes, the tellers and or, some of the tellers did dress in black.

I am so going to leave this alone because technology is shit in my view. Too many damned hackers that pry into people's lives because they can.

Instead of using their skill for the benefit of life, some use their skill for evil, and I am going to leave things as is. I know some hackers will not like me for my thoughts, but it's what it is.

This morning now. No, let's not go there yet. Because I am still mad at the Moon. Trust me; the Moon made sure I saw it in my dream. A bright round moon appeared to me in my dream. And yes, I got mad at the Moon for doing that.

I am mad at the Moon and yes, God, for the lies humans tell on them come on now. Do something to debunk the lies of humans, and not keep shut. Yes, the Blue Moon that I saw, but that Blue Moon is no consolation to me when it comes to the lies of humans; man bout dem walk pan Moon. Which BC Moon?

To me, the Blue Moon that I saw; on this given day is truly not big enough to do the damage I need it to do when it comes to the sins, and lies of humans. Yes, this is my vengeance, and it is truly not right, but I am truly sick, and tired of the lies of White People, and the lies, and deceit they sell globally.

Stop lying to people about space travel because not one White Person know space travel.

Humans have not the technology to travel in time; space. __*If humans did; knew speed, they would know that Mach speed is truly not speed in space; time.*__ Humans are way too gullible because none is looking at it. Earth has a heating, and cooling system therefore; the Moon is Earth's cooling system. So now tell me, if man cannot go to the sun, how the hell can they get to the moon? *Repeating myself I know.*

When did the Moon begin to melt to accommodate human life?

What about vibration?

Can man, or any technology of man vibrate to match speed and time?

Man don't even know the difference between physical time, and spiritual time. That space in time, or time in space when physical time sync with spiritual time.

The human body is made up of energy as well. No. I will not educate you because I know the negative forces in space.

37

Now let me ask you this. Is the Moon man's bitch just like God? Meaning the way man; humans has, and have made God their bitch that bow down to death.

So yes, I am mad at God and the Moon for the lies of men; humans period. Lies they tell on God, the Moon; space.

Trust me, I need to create my own world void of the lies, and sins of man; humans globally, and spiritually including beyond.

Sick of it all. As for my dreams this morning; *I am tired of seeing the nasty world of the English Monarch.*

Why the hell am I seeing the life of Meagan Markle, and her child. ___In the dream she was forcing her son to accept the nasty life she's accepted.___

Family and people; my true family, you will not comprehend this. I know what the dream mean therefore, in the dream; Meagan was a bad mother. You cannot force your child into accepting your nastiness. Therefore, I have to wonder if her mother is a true Jamaican.

No, what has happened to us as Black People?

When did we stop seeing evil?

When did all Jamaicans lose their sight?

You know what let me stop.

I will not get into generational sins, and curses because whether BLACK PEOPLE KNOW IT *ARE NOT, SOME ARE BLEEPED.*

Some truly do not have life therefore, their children cannot have life. **_ONCE YOU SEVER TIES WITH LIFE, YOUR CHILD'S LIFE WITH LIFE; GOD IS SEVERED ALSO._** Therefore, your child cannot have a saving grace when it comes to life. You took life away from that child. So from generation unto generation your off spring, and their off spring, and so forth cannot have life. Death is all they can have therefore, God has, and have become unattainable. And I hope I've explained it right Lovey.

So because this girl has, and have given up life; **_her child cannot have life but death._**

THIS IS HOW I KNOW IT TO BE THEREFORE, I AM TRULY TIRED OF SEEING THE EVILS OF BLACK PEOPLE; WELL WHITE PEOPLE BECAUSE ONCE ANY BLACK PERSON SEVER TIES WITH GOD, THEY DO NOT FALL UNDER THE BANNER OF BLACK; LIFE, THEY FALL UNDER THE BANNER OF WHITE; WHITE DEATH.

This is why too I get mad at God. God has kept his, and her mouth shut when it comes to the truth of life. Yes, you have these books because I was told to write a book, and I've been doing so, but how many has, and have read these books?

People do not want, or need the truth of life. The lies of men suit them fine thus humans globally live by lies. Billions are going to die by lies yet, none know this apart from me.

So yes, I am upset at God, and the Moon for letting the lies of men; humans continue. Thus; evil wanting, and needing a time extension for which I cannot let happen. Like I said; I am tired of seeing into the world of wicked and evil people **_BOTH BLACK AND WHITE IN HUE._**

I need life for myself. I cannot let evil hold on to me. Therefore, this morning my dream world would not let me go of what is happening in this girl's life. **_FROM YOU CHOOSE DEATH, YOU CANNOT HAVE LIFE. DEATH MUST CONTROL YOUR LIFE, AND DEATH MUST KILL YOU._** This is the law of death. _Therefore; despite me being upset at God, and the Moon, I am truly happy, and proud of God that all evil is locked out of life._

I am truly happy, and proud of God that none; not one child of God die to save evil. God would never ever bow to the will of evil; death by sacrificing truth; a child of life to death.

EVIL CHILDREN, AND PEOPLE HAVE TO MAKE SACRIFICES UNTO DEATH THEREFORE; I KNOW WITHOUT DOUBT THAT THE WHITE MAN'S GOD IS TRULY NOT THE GOD OF BLACKS; THE TRUE, AND REAL BLACK RACE.

This many in the Black Community cannot comprehend because their life is based on pagan values; the values of death. And yes, this is why many

40

Blacks kill each other, are jealous of each other, tear down, and rip down each other, uphold pagan values, have the different carnivals globally that glorify death, sin music unto death by glorifying death in their lyrics – see MADABLE SICK by Mad Cobra, and Bounty Killer, make sacrifices unto death, bow down to death in the churches of death globally, and more. Thus many Blacks will forever be loyal to their god who is Death.

So as many Blacks sold out in the days of old; beginning, their off springs continually do the same. Therefore, Satan; Death has many in the Black Community truly locked in hell for real literally.

Yes, their name is permanently locked in the Book of Death; hath no saving grace ever. Therefore, you now know that Death has their DEATH AMBASSADORS' HERE ON EARTH. Yes, many of these MUSICAL ARTISTS.

With death you can do all you want, and get away with it.

Death will keep you, and give you all you want until your appointed time when your spirit leave the flesh. Then your hell begins. Humans truly do not think of this, and this is sad.

Earth did become the domain of death.

Earth did become the state, and resting place of death; the death of flesh.

Earth did become the state, and domain of all that is immoral, and vile.

Earth did become the state, and domain of liars, and thieves.

Murderers
Whores, and prostitutes

Earth herself did become the whore of men; humans because earth is sustaining, and maintaining all that is wicked and evil.

Yes evil is contained on land; but when it comes to the sky, the sky is failing me; life. Man seek to spread their vile, and immoral ways above, and this God, nor the Moon, and sky; heaven can permit.

Evil cannot escape the confines of Earth therefore, the heaven and or, sky need to protect above; the sky and or, heaven better.

As for Cuba. I dreamt Chinese looking Jamaicans wanting to invest in Cuba, but the White Jamaicans were against this venture. They did not want the Chinese looking Jamaicans to invest in Cuba. I intervened, and was for the Chinese looking Jamaicans investing in Cuba. I told them; the Chinese looking Jamaicans to start with the infrastructure of Cuba. I told them, I went there; Cuba, and I gave out books, and pencils to some. I told them the people of Cuba is appreciative of what you give them.

Family and people; my true family. I did go to Cuba, but my experience was not that nice. It was cold, and I almost died there. The people of Cuba, Varadero is extremely nice. Food wise the food was not for me because I am limited with what I can eat. But apart from that, I would invest in Cuba, but I would start with the infrastructure of the land.

I truly love that Cuban land stays in Cuban hands.
The government do not sell the land out to foreign investors therefore, securing the future of their people unlike other lands that sell out land, and people to the highest bidder. Lands like Jamaica, Cayman Islands, all of Africa, and more.

Black People own squat. Not even the skin on our body in my book. Black lands are so poor, and in debt that it's a wonder how the land is still going. *No, they are not going because; the inept drangcrow dem wey run the different BLACK LANDS HAS, AND HAVE TURNED THE PEOPLE INTO BEGGARS, THIEVES, WHORES, AND PROSTITUTES, UNCLEAN BEASTS, IMMORAL CREATURES, AND MORE.*

Therefore, I truly would like to see China investing more in Cuba structure wise. And no, this has absolutely nothing to do with politics with me. The infrastructures in Cuba need proper upgrading.

Yes, I know lands have sided with the United States of America to put sanctions on the land, but why?

Why the hell should anyone bow down, and kiss the ass of America, or any Americans?

Who the bleep are they to dictate to other nations when they can't even govern their own damned people?

Just take a walk in downtown Los Angeles, and you will see what I am talking about.

If I do not have poor relations with a land, I refuse to let any jackass of another land tell me I cannot have positive trade with that nation. I am not your people, or bitch so therefore, truly do not tell me how to conduct my business affairs. I can't tell you how to do business. So, why are you in my business affairs?

I refuse to, and will not side with you to hate anyone. Kiss my natural brown ass bitch.

YOUR ARMIES OF DEATH DOESN'T MAKE YOU POWERFUL. IT JUST MAKES YOU BROKE PHYSICALLY, AND SPIRITUALLY. YES, BROKE AS NIGGAS.

God did not make you overseer of any land therefore, stay your kiss mi ass ground. If we are true friends that deal fairly with each other, and that country pose a threat to you, and your people then yes, I will stay true to our friendship, but otherwise no. I cannot hate anyone because you hate them, and want to dictate, and control them.

Listen, you build nuclear weapons.

Have dropped an Atomic Bomb on another land that are still living with the consequences of your evil actions. Why should I leave my land defenceless?

But then God is my defence so; however the wicked, and evil of the global world kill themselves is truly up to them. *I know your hell therefore; every political leader of the globe*

44

has their spot in hell except for Nelson Mandela. He is saved.

And on that note I am going to stop there.

I was to add the full content of my dream that I put on the back cover of ***MY MORNING THOUGHTS BOOK TWO*** in this book, but I can't find the written version, and I am so lazy to go look for it. So I am going to leave those dreams alone. I am lazy people, and like I said; I am tired of my dream world. Seeing the evils of nasty bitches that have no moral values that are good, and true.

I am tired of the amount of deaths I see via dreams, and my waking state. I need life therefore, I need a true escape from all of this.

Yes, I am looking to go to Africa to meditate for a couple of days, and eat some African food; well organic fruits, and vegetables hopefully.

Can't stand the genetically modified shit that is shoved down our throats to shorten our physical, and spiritual life.

Oh shit I forgot. I dreamt about Koffee, Beenie Man, Ninja Man, and the War Lord, Bounty Killer.

In the dream Koffee changed. You know what forget it. Because in the dream, I was against her because she was truly not cultural. And no, I truly do not listen to her music in real life.

Let it go Michelle.

So, yes, the lies in the musical industry when it comes to Jamaicans continue. Many need to clean their act up because they; the artists are misleading the people, and sending the younger generation further into hell with the lyrical content of their music.

I so will not talk about Corn Flakes and Buddy Wata that many still listen to.

Michelle

It's another day; July 23, 2019, and I so need to end this book. Night started at after 2am which is normal for me. My naps during the day carries me through until early am along with my game play. Farmville people. I am at level 91 now, and truly loving it though at times I get bored of the game.

Sleep was good until I started to dream because it seems Death truly have a hold on me. Death refuse to let me go in this way – sight. Like I said, I am tired, and now I am truly tired of seeing the evils that some do. Family and people; my true family, I refuse to worry about the wicked and evil of this world. I see, and document hence these many books.

If Life; God need a record, trust me; these books are records. What I see via my dream world, and beyond is truly recorded for real.

Now this morning, I was in Russia. I cannot fully remember if the now President of Russia was there. No, he was there though his presence was vague. People were being killed by government officials and or, the police force. I say government officials due to the President of Russia.

Family and people; My true family. I don't know what this guy did, but he was medium build, and naked with a very small and or, small penis. He had no smile on his face because he was worried. He was brought naked before this box. Oh man how do I describe it for you. I would say the opening of the box was square. When you think box, ***think vats where they put the dead.*** I had mine; box and or, burial chamber, and he had his. But the thing is; older women that would seem to be grand mothers were being buried also. I did not go into the box trust me on that. But initially I thought I was going to be raped.

I will not analyze this dream because like I said, Death has a hold on me, and refuse to let me go. I have to see the killings of Death if that makes any sense.

So I truly do not know what disaster is going to affect Russia and or, some European lands that see people die. I will not analyze this dream because I truly do not know why politicians feel the need to dominate, and control; even kill. No, I will wane my anger, and temper because Death want to see me pissed all the time.

I do not need to see death constantly. I need to see life; good, and true life, and attain life; good and true life. *However death kills globally is truly up to death, and not my concern.*

Yes, I want and need to be cold hearted, but I need to live my life. Death can literally kiss my natural brown ass. Keep your people, and do what you will with them but leave me out of the loop. I truly don't care because humans have, and has proven time and time again that they truly do not value life.

Michelle

Had a beautiful sleep this morning. I was up until late playing Farmville, and my game play affected my dream world when it came to the elimination of things.

Oh Lord have mercy, good afternoon everyone. It is July 26, 2019, and I have true life thank God.

Did not dream death yeah me.

Dreamt Phillips, and Peter Bunting. These men are apart of the Jamaican inept. Sorry, Jamaican Government.

In the dream, it was winter though it's summer in the physical world. Where I am at as well as, in Jamaica. In the dream Peter Bunting won the electoral race and became the **_NEW PRIME MINISTER OF JAMAICA._**

His first act of business was severing ties with Canada. In the dream, he was not important when it came to the other leaders of the globe. In the dream, he wanted to be noticed by other leaders especially the Prime Minister, but none noticed him. At any rate, I was over joyed that Bunting; Peter Bunting won and became Prime Minister of Jamaica. But, in the dream; **_I knew he was not going to do anything for the people of Jamaica._**

In the dream, **_all I saw him as was a whore._** He was going to use his office to shell dung the place by; spending lavishly on hairy motels, and hotels. The finances of Jamaica was not his concern just the women he had under his belt that he could shower with lavish things. Expensive trips, cars, and more.

Suh. Nuh betta barrel, nuh betta herring. Another leader plunging Jamaica, and the people of Jamaica further into hell. **_Yes, I thought about his degree in the dream hence,_** _**he could not put his degree to good use for the benefit of his land, and people.**_ I so want to cuss out this man BC, but I will refrain from doing so. Therefore, a pure drangcrow run Jamaica. _**Educated dunce that rape land, and people of their truth, and true wealth.**_ Men that fling dem dick around like a wata hose watering the lawn. Therefore, the whores, and prostitutes that govern the land of Jamaica literally.

Michelle

BOOKS WRITTEN BY MICHELLE JEAN 2019

MY WORLD OF DREAMS 2019 – BOOK ONE

MY WORLD OF DREAMS 2019 – BOOK TWO

MY WORLD OF DREAMS 2019 – BOOK THREE

MY WORLD OF DREAMS 2019 – BOOK FOUR

A LITTLE TALK 2019

JUST ONE OF THOSE DAYS 2019

A LITTLE TALK 2019 – BOOK TWO

MY TALK 2019

CHANGES

MY WORLD OF DREAMS 2019 – BOOK FIVE

MY WORLD OF DREAMS 2019 – BOOK SIX

MY WORLD OF DREAMS 2019 – BOOK SEVEN

MY WORLD OF DREAMS 2019 – BOOK EIGHT

MY MORNING THOUGHTS – BOOK ONE

MY MORNING THOUGHTS – BOOK TWO